SHOW US THE MONEY!

A BEGINNER'S GUIDE TO WEATLH BUILDING TODAY AND FOR FUTURE GENERATIONS

What every African American should know about investing

Published by BHE
P.O. Box 773
Bridgeton, MO 63044

Printed in the United States of America

The information provided within this guide is for general informational purposes only. While the author tries to keep the information up-to-date and correct, there are no representations or warranties, express or implied, about the completeness, accuracy, reliability, suitability or availability with respect to the information, products, services, or related graphics contained in this book for any purpose. Any use of this information is at your own risk.

Disclaimer: Nothing published in this guide should be considered personalized investment advice. Although general information is being provided, the author is not licensed under securities laws to address your particular investment situation. Any investments made should be by choice or made after consulting with an investment advisor who is licensed in securities.

ISBN 10: 1544073534
ISBN 13: 9781544073538

INTRODUCTION

Can you feel it? I most certainly do. America is rapidly changing, and when it pertains to the wealth gap in this country, African Americans are falling way behind. Many reasons revolve around a toxic combination of institutionalized discrimination, racism, and policies put forth by the government which heightens inequality. There is also no question that history, slavery in particular, created the gap. Wealth has always been unequally distributed in this country, and other races have benefited tremendously.

Before I share with you my suggestions about what we can do to start closing the gap and build wealth, I need to share some simple facts that may sting a little. According to the Institute for Policy Studies, white households own, on average, seven times as much wealth as African Americans. The *Forbes* 100 top billionaires are collectively as rich as all black Americans combined. It would take us more than 200 years to have as much wealth as our white counterparts. That's a hard pill to swallow, but it is, indeed, our reality.

Another thing that may shock you is the poverty rate for African Americans is at 27%, an all-time high. Our median household income is $36,898, significantly lower than our white counterparts with a median household income of $62,950. Forty-five percent of African American children, under the age of six, live in poverty. Let me repeat . . . 45% of our children under six, live in DEEP poverty! Even with similar educational backgrounds as whites, black people earn between 12-20 percent less than whites. Again, these are the facts and they are our reality. Nonetheless, my question to everyone reading this is . . . what are we going to do about it? Are we going to sit idly by and let those numbers increase? Complaining surely won't change our current status, nor will spending money on unnecessary items that continue to swell the pockets of rich people. I cannot express the amount of money I've wasted over the years on complete nonsense—I'm sure many of you can attest to wasting money too. Now that the money is long gone, let's take a deep breath and consider this tad bit of information a wake-up call.

While the facts above may be disputed by some and ignored by others, here is the truth. If we want to close the wealth gap and get on a secure path to prosperity, we have to get serious about growing money and investing. There are always certain risks involved with investing, but with the stock market at record highs, this is a risk you may want to consider.

With that being said, I would like to tell you a few things about me, and convey why I truly believe now is the time for many more African Americans to delve into the stock market. First, I totally understand the skepticism many of you may have. Not only that, but let's be real honest with each other. Many things that revolve around the stock market seem so foreign to us. We have no clue what purpose the stock market serves, and if you ask, many people wouldn't be able to tell you what the Dow Jones Industrial Average, Nasdaq or S&P 500 are all about. I surely didn't know, until I started working for a brokerage firm, Cutter & Company Investments, years ago in St. Louis. At the time, I was an insurance broker. I wanted to learn more about securities, especially since nearly everyone there was involved, one way or another. But my idea of "learning" resulted in little research and setting up a trading account with $500. I purchased multiple shares of stock from ONE company and invested in mutual funds. Many of my coworkers raved about a particular company that was on the rise, and right before I went all in, the company's stock soared to nearly 308%. I was ecstatic! On a daily basis I watched my stock fluctuate up and down, hoping and praying that it would present more gains and allow me to purchase the beachfront property I always wanted and retire at the young age of thirty. Well, unfortunately, that never happened. Eventually, the stock plummeted and I was back to square one. I vowed to never invest in the stock market again, and right after I quit my job to pursue a writing career and start my own insurance business, Hampton Insurance Agency, I cashed out my mutual funds, in fear of losing that money too. So when people mention to me their fears of losing money in the stock market, I totally get it. But the truth is, nothing was guaranteed and I honestly should have done my homework. Investing in ONE company was not the route to go, and I didn't know any specifics about the company I invested in. I just went with the flow, which was a very bad move on my part.

As with anything you do, research always helps. I'm not going to tell you which stocks or mutual funds I think you should invest in—that will be totally up to you. What I will say, however, is this. Opening an online broker account for trading purposes is a very good start. This will enable you to directly buy and sell everything from stocks and bonds to mutual funds. Over the long term, the return on a diversified portfolio is greater than simply having a savings account. You are the one in control, and you can make trade transactions right from your own computer.

Why now? Well, if you haven't noticed, the stock market is at an all-time high. Many companies are showing optimism for the future and with so many new innovations on the horizon, particularly in technology, health, agriculture, energy, commodities . . . now is the time for you to plant a tiny seed and watch it grow. Keep in mind that you don't have to invest all of your money into stocks and you can start with very little cash. You also don't have to wear your wealth, and the notion that people need to *see* your wealthy status on you is nonsense. It's nice to have the finer things in life, but be smart about your finances. Start utilizing your money so that it can benefit you in the long run, and know that being frugal isn't necessarily a bad thing at all. There is no secret that we are conditioned to spend rather than to invest. It's time to break that cycle. There's been a divisive agenda to keep us in the dark—one that has prohibited us from getting ahead and implementing ideas that truly strengthen the black community. Teaching our youth how to invest is one of the best ways forward. I cannot stress this enough, and as you create your own portfolio, be sure to encourage your family and friends to create one as well.

As a national bestselling author, I've been fortunate enough to save money throughout the years. Not nearly as much as I would've liked to, and when unforeseen expenses arise, I often see some of those funds trickle down to very little. Getting ahead seems nearly impossible, but it wasn't until a few years ago when I realized that GROWING my money was just as vital as saving it. I started to examine the fastest way to grow money. That was when I discovered that one of my biggest mistakes was not investing in the stock market. Fear of losing money had consumed my mind, and I just didn't want to take the risk again. This time, however, the research I'd done, along with the information I received, provided a real sense of understanding how the market actually worked. I immediately started to see gains that I never thought were possible. Gains that have grown over time and now have me wondering why in the heck I waited so long. Especially, since self-employed individuals, like me, don't have employers who contribute to their 401(k) plans or who involuntarily include their employees in investment plans. Even so, many people living paycheck-to-paycheck find themselves borrowing against their retirement and still not being able to have a sizeable amount of money left for retirement. That's why it's important to maintain a diversified portfolio of your own—one that you can have easy access to, and when certain trends start to arise, you can get on board and start allowing your money to work for you. That's exactly what I did, and how I got started was pretty simple. I'm going to share with you some basic information about investing. What I want you to understand is this is not a get-rich-quick guide. It's not a scam either, and no one is paying me anything to share this information with you. It is my attempt to get more African Americans invested in the stock market, to encourage you to start building wealth for yourself and generations to come, and to help us close the wealth gap between blacks and whites. If you are willing to receive this information, and do the research, you will embark upon a life-changing experience that'll have you wondering, too, why you waited so long to get started.

BASIC THINGS YOU SHOULD KNOW...

What is the stock market and how does it work?

A simple definition: The stock market is a place where stocks and bonds are traded. It allows investors to partake in the financial achievements of the company's shares they hold. For instance, when you buy a stock, you become a shareholder. You own "part" of the company; therefore, if the company's profits increase, you share the profits. On the other hand, if profits drop, so does the price of your stock. How you lose is if/when the stock falls below the price you paid for it. Over time, the goal is to grow small sums of money into large ones. By allowing organizations and individuals, like you and me, to invest and participate in the financial achievements of these companies, it is a way to generate wealth.

Stocks-Stocks represent a claim on a company's assets and earnings. It is a share in ownership of the company.

Bonds-Bonds are debt investments where the investor loans money to an entity who borrows funds for a period of time at a variable or fixed interest rate.

Mutual Funds-A company that pools money from multiple investors to invest in stocks, bonds and other securities.

Diverse Portfolio-Mixing a variety of investments within a portfolio.

Trade-Buying or selling.

Stock Symbols-A unique series of letters that identify a company on the stock exchange.

Shares-Shares are the units of investment in individual companies.

Shareholder-An owner of shares in a company.

After you open an online trading account, one of the first things you will see is symbols like: NYSE, NDAQ, DJIA and S&P 500. Many of us see these symbols often, but don't necessarily know what they represent. The New York Stock Exchange (NYSE) is considered the largest equities-based exchange in the world, located at 11 Wall Street in New York. It's open for trading Monday through Friday, 9:30 a.m. to 4:00 p.m. EST, with the exception of holidays. During those hours, traders can execute stock transactions on behalf of investors, many times electronically. Years ago, you couldn't trade without a broker. Now, you can have access to the market through online trading. After you make a trading transaction, a broker on the other end still has to facilitate your order. Still, you can virtually trade without speaking to anyone. In most cases, there are fees involved in online trading and some brokers earn small commissions on each trade.

Nasdaq (NDAQ) is considered the second largest exchange in the world, located in Times Square. It is a global electronic marketplace for buying and selling securities, and is a benchmark operations index for U.S. Tech stocks. The difference between the two exchanges is their trading practices. The NYSE is an auction market; the Nasdaq is a dealer's market.

Dow Jones Industrial Average (DJIA) is an index of the largest business and financial companies with significant stocks traded on the NYSE. All companies have household names with proven track records of success. Some of these companies include: Apple, General Electric, Exxon Mobil Corporation, Microsoft, Walmart and Walt Disney. If the Dow is up, usually, that means these companies are doing quite well.

Standard & Poor's 500 Index (S&P 500) is an index of 500 stocks, chosen by economists, seen as a leading indicator of equities in the U.S. It is a better indication of how the market is operating, simply because it includes 500 companies, instead of 30 companies that represent the Dow.

What most of us know about Wall Street is what we hear in the news. To say the least, the news often delivers daunting information that warns us to stand clear. In addition to that, many of us remember what happened during the 2007-2008 global financial crisis. It was deemed the worst financial crisis since the great depression, one that our country will never forget. Wall Street is known as a culture that breeds greed. The bonuses hedge fund managers and traders receive are jaw dropping. The obsession with money making is real, and the selfish mentality of many individuals is what brought about the financial crisis. The Dodd-Frank Wall Street Reform and Consumer Protection Act was designed to regulate Wall Street. It was signed by President Obama on July 21, 2010, but many individuals believe that Wall Street can never be truly regulated and the environment remains the same. During the financial crisis, in one day, the market fell 777.68 points. It was the largest drop in a single day, in history. Many investors lost money during this period, retirement accounts were depleted and home foreclosures had risen to a level this nation had never seen. Also during this period, investors who could still afford to invest mustered the storm and made millions when the markets recovered and bounced back. Many stocks were at an all-time low, and had I known what I know today, I would have jumped right in. Unfortunately, I truly believe this period was a missed opportunity for African Americans to start wealth building.

Nevertheless, I'm ready! I'm inspired by stories I hear, pertaining to investors making huge profits after a company goes public on the stock exchange. These stories should excite all of us, and one that is so impressive to me is Netflix(NFLX). Netflix was one of the first-moving companies to stream videos over the internet. Many people didn't believe it could be done, but Netflix found investors who were willing to take a chance on them. They went public on the stock exchange in 2002, and at the time, their IPO (Initial Public Offering) was $15 per share. Within a short period, they had gains of nearly 8,000 percent. So, if you would have invested $1,000, you would have profited $81,000. If you would have invested $10,000, your profit would have been $810,000. It may seem like a lot of money to invest, but it sure did pay off for investors. As with any company, Netflix experienced a downturn where investors were able to buy stock in their company for less than $5 a share. Netflix reinvented the company, and it wasn't long before investors saw even bigger profits. As of today, Netflix shares are trading around $142. Can you imagine the amount of money investors have made over the years? I can only wonder how many of those investors are African American.

Amazon also has an impressive story. When Jeff Bezo started Amazon, yet again, many people didn't quite see the vision. Some, however, did and they became investors. Investors who paid $18.00 per share in 1997, when the company went public. Today, Amazon's stock is trading around $856 a share! Yes, I said it . . . $856 per share! Investors have benefited from explosive gains of nearly 48,000 percent! Can you do the math? I mean, how would you like to have a piece of that pie!

There are many stock history stories to tell, and if you can't afford to own 900 million in shares of Walmart, like

Warren Buffett does, then consider pooling your funds with people you trust. Buffett recently sold 90% of his Walmart shares, but my point is, even though you may never have Warren Buffett's money to purchase that many shares, maybe by pooling money to buy high-dollar stocks like Netflix or Amazon isn't such a bad idea. I certainly can't predict what the future holds for either of those companies, but I do know there are companies just like those on the stock exchange, seeking investors like you and me.

In relations to the stock market, the goal is to invest in companies when they're at the innovation stage. Right after the innovation stage they reach the acceptance stage (see chart). This is a good time to enter as well, but it only means that time may be running out. By the time a company reaches the saturation stage, it may be too late to invest. The shares are so high that they may be difficult to afford.

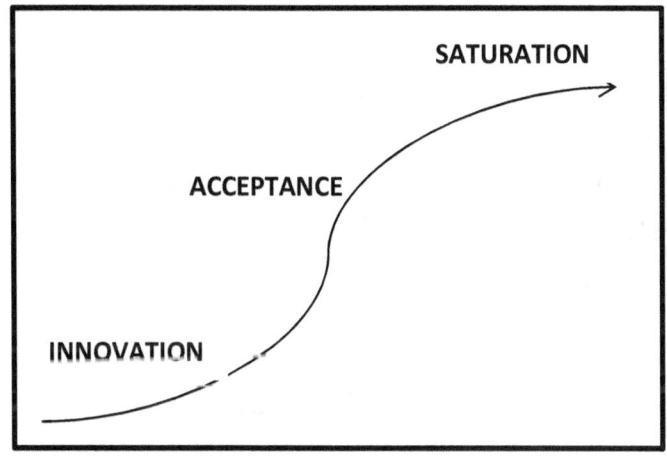

The last thing I want to point out in this chapter is the chart you'll see, once you open a trading account and start investing. Basically, what do those squiggly lines mean and what do the colors imply? Well, green is positive, red is negative. Those squiggly lines represent stages of your stock.

Stage 1 is right after a prolonged downtrend. The stock is trading sideways, and sellers are beginning to lose their power. This is the worst position to be in. Many investors hold their breaths, hoping for a quick turnaround.

Stage 2 is where the uptrend begins and it is also known as the break-out stage. The majority of money is made at this stage. Many investors accumulate as many shares as possible and prepare for stage 3.

Stage 3 is where stocks start to trade sideways again. Because profits look pretty good at this stage, some investors pull out. Beginners, however, start to dig in because they view a company as profitable. The opportunity to make a profit at this point may be too late. Always try to get in at stage 2, if you can.

Stage 4 is the dreaded downtrend, especially for those who are willing to wait it out and see what happens. Many times stocks bounce back, sometimes they don't.

As you start to invest in the stock market and you begin to receive information from individuals about which stocks to buy, which ones will explode or why you need to purchase this particular stock NOW, please know that NO ONE can really predict what stocks will do or how fast they will grow your money. And even after doing all the research you can do, you still may not feel comfortable purchasing a particular stock. Most people, however, take chances. Investing in the stock market is a risky business, so please be sure to recognize your tolerance risk level.

LETTING GO OF YOUR FEARS

Why blacks don't invest?

There are many reasons why African Americans don't invest. I shared my reason for vowing to never invest again, and at the time, I thought it made much sense. As I started to converse with others about why they don't invest, I discovered several reasons listed below, in no particular order.

1) Too risky
2) Lack of knowledge about how the stock market works
3) No money to invest
4) Fear of trying something new
5) Some view the stock market as a scam
6) Would rather invest in real estate, something they can see, touch or feel
7) Don't have time
8) Believe the stock market is only beneficial to other races
9) Cost too much to invest
10)   Can't find a trustworthy broker

So, there you have it. Ask any black person why they don't invest, nine times out of ten their reason can be found on this list. What I'd like to do is tackle one issue at a time, starting with taking risks.

It is a fact that taking risks can lead to success. Any successful entrepreneur will tell you that they didn't accomplish many of their goals without taking *some* risks. So why do we often view risk-taking in a negative light? I'm not sure. It is evident that some risks never pay off, but the majority of risks do. It shows that you fully believe in what you're seeking to accomplish, and you're optimistic about the outcome. You also learn valuable lessons along the way, and if you fail, try again. In reference to the stock market, start small. At least be willing to see how things work. After you feel comfortable, relax and invest more.

The lack of knowledge about the stock market was one of the main reasons I'd heard, as to why blacks don't want to invest. I truly understand this, and even when I started my research, I felt like a complete idiot. But day by day, it started to sink in. I made time to learn what I needed to know about growing wealth, and anyone willing to share information with me through videos (Dr. Boyce Watkins) or books, I was certainly all in. As with anything, you have to be willing to learn, and, possibly learn on your own. Unfortunately, learning about the stock market was one of those things where many blacks felt shut out. Basically, if it wasn't being taught in school, we assumed we didn't need to know about it. As we all know now, there was a substantial amount of vital subjects that weren't taught to us in school, but we desperately needed to know about them. How the stock market operates is one of those things. Because it revolves around wealth building, we really do need to know and learn as much information as possible. After all—I'm sure you've heard this plenty of times before, but I'll say it again. Knowledge is power.

If you have no money to invest, yes, I feel your pain. But when you get serious about investing, trust me, the money is there. What I'm about to tell you is a true story. A few years ago, I decided to experiment with online trading. I was fearful of using the money in my savings, along with money I'd earned from writing—you already know my experience at Cutter & Company left me with a bad taste in my mouth about investing. So what I did was search for "extra" change around the house and inside of our vehicles. I even sold a few items that I didn't need anymore, and I encouraged my children to do the same. When all was said and done, we came up with approximately eight hundred dollars. I never would have guessed that the middle compartment in my car had twelve dollars in change in it, and the change my husband had been compiling in a drawer added to the total. We emptied our piggy banks, and every penny that we found went toward our investment efforts. After I had my investment funds, I opened an account with an online broker that had no minimum startup cost. I knew I had to put in money to invest, so I started my account with $60. Through research, I'd heard some interesting things about penny stocks, so I decided to start there. And within two weeks, I was totally shocked by the gains. There were losses as well, but overall, and as I started to create a more diverse portfolio, things started to look better and better. Eventually, I increased my amount for investing, and as I said from the beginning, I can only wonder why I hadn't done this sooner. My suggestion to you is, find the money. Start small and cutback where you can. Weigh your needs and wants. And trust me when I say many of us are not as broke as we believe.

Fear of investing is probably one of the items listed above that I really don't understand. Simply because you're the one in control of your investments. You decide how much you're willing to spend in the stock market, and how much you can tolerate to possibly lose. I guess, for some, there is the fear of trying something new. We're afraid to step out of our comfort zones, and whenever anyone presents us with ideas about how to make more money, we tend to brush it off. I'm sure there will be plenty of people who read this guide just to dispute everything I've said and attempt to discourage you. Then there will be those who find themselves willing to invest for the first time and finally commit to building wealth. To those individuals, pat yourselves on the back. You're on the right track.

The stock market is not a scam, but I assure you that there are plenty of scammers in this world, who create scams relating to the stock market. Many of you may have seen the movie *The Wolf of Wall Street*, starring Leonardo DiCaprio. Or, maybe, you've heard of Bernard "Bernie" Madoff, a former stockbroker and investment advisor who created a Ponzi scheme that was considered the largest financial fraud in U.S. history. In both cases, investors lost billions, not millions, but billions. Madoff is currently serving time in prison, but many of the investors he swindled have yet to recover their money. There are numerous scammers out there, and you have to be careful when people approach you about things that sound too good to be true. One reason I refuse to provide specificities about the dollar amount of my portfolio is because the amount every investor makes will be different. I never want you to believe that you can accumulate more or less than I do, and providing you with such information would be misleading. I want you to create your own portfolio and invest at a level that feels suitable for you. If you decide to ultimately work with a broker, just be sure to examine his/her background and don't forget to ask for many references.

There is no other way to put this, other than to say investing in real estate is a smart move! I've done so myself, and owning a piece of land feels pretty darn good. But what do you think enabled me to invest in real estate? How do you think I was able to generate enough money to buy property and make a profit? Five words. Investing in the stock market. See, when it comes to investing, eventually, you'll need to have your hands in everything. Don't allow other people to make all the money, and when you hear bright ideas about investing, don't be so quick to say no. Just a small investment in a project can turn out to be huge in the long run. You have to start somewhere, and when I start to present more investment opportunities in the near future, I hope you'll give it much consideration. A big mistake is believing that we need to wear our wealth on us for people to see is not wise. Either we're going to own something or be owned. Now is the time to make smarter choices, so let's get busy in a major way and wealth build together.

If you think you don't have time to invest, basically, what you're saying is you don't have time to make money. I don't know of anyone who doesn't want to make money, so find the time and do the research.

One may assume that the stock market is for whites in particular, simply because they are the ones who have benefited the most from it, especially college educated whites who are already financially stable. But why is that? The reason is because many African Americans do not invest. The stock market could be beneficial to us, too. There is a possibility that we could see some of the same gains as our white counterparts. We have every opportunity to close the wealth gap and turn around some of those horrific stats about our income. I mean, why are so many of us okay with being/falling behind in every statistic pertaining to wealth? We know there are reasons why things are the way they are—many reasons have been beyond our control. But we can no longer allow those things to hold us back. As you look at your children, think about them and generations to come. Wouldn't it be nice if you were the one who finally made a decision to start wealth building for your family?

If you're ready, start your computers and let's get ready for some trade action!

GETTING STARTED . . .

How to buy stocks online?

If you've made it this far in the book, I assume you're interested in investing or you're just about ready. There are multiple online brokers you can use for trading, but I'm only going to provide you with information from the ones I view as the top five for beginners. Please do your homework on each one of them, before deciding which one you want to use. Many charge fees for trading—some are higher than others. Some will do robust research for you, others will send you videos to watch about investing and are available around-the-clock, in case you have any questions. All of them offer advanced trading platforms, and some have no inactivity fees, in case you need to take a break from the ups and downs in the stock market. Most have local branches, if you prefer to go into an office and speak to someone. I can tell you that my experience with the online brokerage firm I chose has been nothing but great. Can you guess which one it is?

Scottrade is a privately owned brokerage firm with online and retail locations. It was founded in 1980 by Roger O. Riney, and headquarters are located in St. Louis, MO. The company's revenue is 1.1 billion. They offer an array of online tools to get you started. Current commission rate is $7 per trade, account minimum is $600. Promotions are available.

TD Ameritrade is a broker based online company, founded in 1975 by Joe Ricketts. Its headquarters is in Omaha, NE and the company's revenue is 3.2 billion. They also offer an abundance of tools to get you started and current commission rate is $6.95 per trade. There is NO account minimum, making this firm very attractive to beginners. Promotions are available.

*Charles*Schwab is an American brokerage and banking company, founded by Charles R. Schwab in 1971. The company's headquarters are in San Francisco, CA. They believe in making their customers healthy and wealthy. Their revenue is 6 billion dollars, and current commission rate is $6.95 per trade. Account minimum is $1,000. Promotions are available.

E*Trade is a financial services company, founded in 1982 by Bernard A. Newcomb and William A. Porter. The company's headquarters is in New York, revenue is 1.4 billion. They specialize in building wealth and want every customer to make long-term investments that can prove to be beneficial in the long run. Current trade commission rate is $9.99 per trade, $500 account minimum. Promotions are available.

OpenHouse is an affiliation of E*Trade. Current commission rate is $4.95 per trade (some of the lowest in the industry). There is no minimum account balance required. If you're an advanced trader, this platform may not be suitable for you because it doesn't offer a clean, modern web-based trading application.

Opening an account with an online broker is simple. What you'll need to provide is:

-Social Security Number or Individual Taxpayer ID

-Employer Name & Address

-Ten or fifteen minutes of your time to complete an application

-Minimum of $0-$5,000, depending on which brokerage firm you choose to use for trading

You can make deposits into your trading account via check, wire transfers or wire deposits. Be sure to check how long it takes before funds are available in your account. Long periods and not having enough funds in your account can prohibit you from investing right away and purchasing stocks when they're at their lowest.

A few important things you should know about a company before you invest:

1) Know and get an understanding of what the company does.
2) Know who the executive officers are and find out an overview of their backgrounds.
3) Know the company's revenue and check how long the company has been in business.
4) Know what strategy they use to maximize their profits. Also, find out if they're competitive with other companies in the same field.
5) Know what their profit margins are, after expenses.
6) Find out how much debt the company has.

JUST SO YOU KNOW . . .

Penny Stocks

If you know a little something about investing, you've probably heard of penny stocks. Some investors claim to have made millions from penny stocks, others have lost money and view them as scams. My experience with penny stocks can be summed up as interesting. Sometimes they're up way high, sometimes they're down. Many times I have made sizeable profits, but because I never view penny stocks as long term, I've cashed out and invested elsewhere.

In general, penny stocks are stocks that belong to small companies that are evolving. Specific details about these companies are vague, and it is difficult to find out everything you need to know. In some cases, you can find out financial information online. Search income statements, revenue & balance sheets. Always be cautious because many of these companies hire savvy writers and industry professionals to create newsletters and articles that rave about the company's success, just to lure you in and get you to invest. Again, if it sounds too good to be true, maybe it is.

Additional things you should know before investing in penny stocks is they trade infrequently. Therefore, it may be difficult to sell your shares, once you've purchased them. These companies aren't traded on the NYSE or Nasdaq, but online trading firms make them available over-the-counter (OTC). This is a method where the buyer and seller deal with each other, without a middle man. I'll stress, again, how cheap these stocks are. You can put yourself in position to see enormous gains. The downside is the demand for them isn't high, so you may have difficulties finding buyers when you want to sell. That's why penny stocks are considered high-risk investments. And while all investments are risky, you stand a better chance of getting ahead by maintaining a diverse portfolio. One that includes a variety of stocks, bonds and mutual funds.

Be sure to check your investments on a daily basis, with the exception of weekends and holidays, when the stock exchange is closed. You'll start to notice key patterns that will indicate when you should buy or sell. For stock updates, check online news sites, join financial groups on social media or read the financial section of any newspaper. Here is a short list of subjects and new innovations, pertaining to stocks, to research:

Gold

Cannabis (Marijuana)

MEMS Chips

Internet of Things

Solar Energy

Drones

Pharmaceutical

Manufacturing

Healthcare

Robots

Automobile

Tech stocks

Radio One

PunchTV

Ready, set, go . . .

This guide is short and sweet, mainly because the last thing I want to do is overwhelm beginning investors with too much information to process. Some of this information you may have already known, but you may be surprised to discover that many people do not know the basics when it comes to investing in the stock market. I hope this information has been valuable to you in every way. More than anything, I hope you're ready to start trading through an online broker. Remember to create a diverse portfolio and start off small. As you see progress, move to the next level and increase your investment amount.

If you're not quite ready to open an account yet, make a commitment to start saving. House/car clean for change and sell some of the things in your home that you don't really need. See how much you can save and ask family/friends you trust to save with you. At the end of the year, pool your funds together and come up with a plan to invest. It could be in real estate or in a business you've been thinking about for years. Share this guide with African American young men and women, particularly seniors in high school or college students. It's never too early to learn the basics about investing; kids need to know about building wealth too. This is how we can begin to close the wealth gap and transition more of our children from poverty to being wealthy. You have to start somewhere, and as we see our country slipping in a new direction, why not start now?

THREE CHALLENGES BEFORE YOU GO

Challenge One: I already mentioned house/car cleaning for change, but this is something else I would like for you to do. There are seven days in a week, right? You choose which day you want to start, but on the first day save one dollar. On the second day save two dollars, third day three, fourth day four, fifth day five, sixth day six and seventh day seven. Then, start all over again—first day, one dollar. Each week you'll save a minimum of $28. Invite everyone in your household to partake in the savings challenge, and if you feel comfortable doubling your daily amounts, please do! See how much you can save as a family and deposit your funds into a savings account so you don't dig into it. Keep me posted on how you're doing throughout the year. My goal is to get, at least, 100 families involved in saving more money by the end of this year. I may even have something special for the family who has saved the most, so don't forget to email updates!

Challenge Two: When it comes to money, I know it's difficult to find people you can trust. But, sometimes, we just can't do it all alone. See if you can find three to five people to pool your money with. Either make a commitment to save or open an online broker account to invest. Create a small business plan with your partners. Even if it takes a few years to generate enough capital for your business, at least you'll all be working toward a common goal. I would love to hear about some of your business ventures, so keep me in the loop! Will we be able to start 50 new black-owned businesses this year? I think we can reach that number and more!

Challenge Three: This is simple. The goal is to get 100 African Americans to open an online broker account before the end of this year. Can we do it? Are you going to invite others to learn about investing and get started? I hope so.

Lastly, be sure to share your thoughts about this guide on Amazon. I want to know if you're ready to start wealth building or if you're still on the fence. In the near future, I'll be seeking serious investors who are interested in pooling funds together to pursue business ventures that will benefit African Americans. We can create a Black Wall Street for sure, but we have to know and understand the basics of investing and growing our money first. Feel free to send any inquiries to brendahampton_1@netzero.net. Put the word investing or saving in the subject line; I'll respond at my earliest convenience. As always . . . I'm rooting for you!

About the Author

A born entrepreneur, Brenda M. Hampton is a native St. Louisan with a broad vision for business. In 1998, she managed Hampton Insurance Agency, an insurance brokerage firm that accommodated many customers throughout Missouri. She retired from the insurance industry in 2001 to pursue a writing career; a career that has led to Hampton being the recipient of numerous awards and honors as a national bestselling author. With more than thirty-plus novels in print, Hampton has accumulated an enormous, dedicated fan base that has grown to appreciate her unique writing, as well as her savvy business ventures, including Brenda Hampton Entertainment. BHE is a reputable brand revolving around all things in the entertainment arena. She created The Brenda Hampton Honorary Literacy Award and Scholarship Fund to not only celebrate writers, but to also award skilled individuals who put forth every effort to uphold the standards of African American literature. Her novels include: *The Naughty Series*, *BFF's Series*, *Hell House Series*, *Full-Figured Series*, *Black President Series* and more stand-a-lone novels, including *In My Shoes*, the story of how she was a teenage mother with twins who distanced herself from the welfare system and found success. Additional information about the author can be found at www.brendamhampton.com.

www.ingramcontent.com/pod-product-compliance
Lightning Source LLC
Chambersburg PA
CBHW051824170526
45167CB00005B/2152